I0146213

Emanuel Geibel

The Wooing of King Sigurd

And the Ballad of the Page and the King's Daughter

Emanuel Geibel

The Wooing of King Sigurd
And the Ballad of the Page and the King's Daughter

ISBN/EAN: 9783744797719

Printed in Europe, USA, Canada, Australia, Japan

Cover: Foto ©Thomas Meinert / pixelio.de

More available books at **www.hansebooks.com**

THE

WOOING OF KING SIGURD,

AND THE BALLAD OF THE

PAGE AND THE KING'S

DAUGHTER.

TRANSLATED FROM GEIBEL BY

ELLEN COOK.

ILLUSTRATIONS BY M. B. AND M. I. B.,

LITHOGRAPHED BY M. I. BOOTH.

SECOND EDITION.

LONDON:

BELL AND DALDY, 186, FLEET STREET.

1864.

THE BALLAD OF THE KING SIGURD.

King Sigurd's Bridal Voyage.

I.

THE spring had come. No more the snow-drifts stood
    On the hill sides; sweet violets fill'd the wood;
The blue waves danced along, from ice set free,
When grey-hair'd king Sigurd put forth to sea.

II.

He spread his sails from far Upsala's strand,
Coasting along the shore, from land to land,
To levy gifts, and use the ancient right
That each should take what best him pleased,—by might.

III.

The ninth morn on their voyage gaily laugh'd,
Each skald and knight his first carouse had quaff'd,
'Midst sails and cordage May winds softly play'd,
When on a smiling shore their course they stay'd.

The Ballad of the King Sigurd.

IV.

Thus ſpake the king, when on the land they ſtood—
" So joyful beats my heart, ſo light my mood,
" I know not if the ſpring-tide makes me gay,
" Or our good wine—a youth I feel to-day."

V.

Further they ſtrode along the yellow ſand,
On booty bent; when lo! a lovely band
Of merry girls to waſh their garments troop'd,
To where ſome elders o'er a brooklet ſtoop'd.

VI.

Gaily they work'd, and ſang in ſportive mood
Over their toil; their miſtreſs by them ſtood,
A maiden fair, who on her mantle wore
A jewell'd claſp; her wriſt a falcon bore.

VII.

In her ſweet youth ſhe ſtood, her roſy face
Beam'd like the early morn; with wondrous grace
Her golden curls fell o'er her girliſh form,
And put the ſhining of her claſp to ſcorn.

VIII.

Then, deeply muſing, ſpake the king Sigurd:
" A lovely maiden, by my royal word!
" Spite of my age, her for my bride I'll take"—
He thought—" or ſure for love my heart will break."

The Ballad of the King Sigurd.

IX.

Then to his ſkalds—" Who is the maid? how named ?"
" The child, oh king! of Alf the Wiſe, far famed ;
" Alfsonnè is her name, becauſe her hair
" Gleams golden as the ſunſhine, and as fair.

X.

" For matchleſs purity the maiden's known,
" Two brothers guard her honour as their own,
" Called Alfblond-bart and Eric Harfenſhall,
" Since Alf the Wiſe feaſts in Valhalla's hall."

XI.

Then thus the king—" Bleſt be the hour, fair maid,
" When, led by love, thy ſteps by me have ſtay'd :
" Ah! might I beg thee, ſweeteſt one, to bring
" A draught of water from that cryſtal ſpring? "

XII.

Alfsonnè ran and fill'd, the veſſel brought ;
Slowly king Sigurd drank, as thus he thought :
" Here quaff I love and youth."   Old fool, and vain !
To dream ſuch treaſures can be thine again !

XIII.

Then ſmiling ſpake he—" Thanks to thee I owe
" For this cool draught ; but ſweeter drink, I know,
" The red wine ſparkling on thy roſy lip,—
" Banquet for gods, love from ſuch mouth to ſip.

XIV.

" By day and night how gladly would I taſte
" Such draughts divine."   Then angrily, in haſte
Spake, red with ſhame and ſcorn, the lovely maid:
" I ſee thou art a ſtranger hither ſtray'd :

XV.

" A noble damſel doſt thou dare accoſt
" As ſome baſe hireling to all virtue loſt ?
" Such wanton trifling, wert thou e'en a king,
" Would foul diſhonour on thy grey beard bring."

XVI.

Then, in her anger, down the ſtream ſhe threw
Her water jar ; the ſhatter'd fragments ſtrew
The flinty bed ; whilſt ſhe, like ſnow-white hind,
Fled ſwift along the banks, fleet as the wind

XVII.

Follow'd her bird.   Amazed ſtood Sigurd there,
Till then he had not deem'd ſhe was ſo fair ;
Stroking his beard he cried in accents ſtern—
" To Alfheim, warriors ! now our ſteps we turn."

The Ballad of the King Sigurd.

How King Sigurd came to Alfheim.

I.

GAY banners waved from Alfheim's ancient walls,
The time was May, and mufic fill'd the halls,
When news was brought, which ftartled every
ear,
That king Sigurd from the fea fhore drew near.

II.

They ftrode to meet him from their caftle's wall,
Thofe two brave heroes, Eric Harfenfhall
And Alfblond-bart; not joyful was their mood,
Their fifter's danger well they underftood.

III.

Upon the bridge they ftay'd to council take:
" A dream dream'd I laft night," young Eric fpake;
" I faw a kingly vulture from aloft
" Swoop down upon a white dove, fair and foft.

IV.

" The fnow-white dove I fhelter'd in my breaft,
" The vulture ftill his fell defign hard prefs'd
" And kill'd the dove, which, brother mine, I fear
" Was our Alfsonn'—the vulture, Sigurd here.

v.

" How fhall we guard her, if he feeks the maid ?"
" Wear we our fwords for nought ?" Alfblond-bart faid;
" Our fhields and corflets ? ne'er fhall our fweet May
" In the cold arms of aged winter lay."

vi.

Whilft thus they fpoke, arofe a wild fhrill found
Of cymbals, trumpets, from the plains around;
Amidft his warriors king Sigurd draws near,
In feftal garments all his train appear.

vii.

Upon the bridge where Alfheim's banners fwell'd
Came Alf to meet him; in his hand he held
A golden cup with jewels on the rim,
And fill'd with coftly wine e'en to the brim.

viii.

With homage due the grey-hair'd king he meets,
His prefence with the loving-cup he greets;
Low bow the men of Alf's and Eric's houfe:
He takes the cup, but drinks no deep caroufe.

ix.

" I will not drink nor reft me by your fires,"
He faid, " till I have told my heart's defires:
" My head is grey, but rich my court and rare,
" A golden crown is worth your golden hair.

The Ballad of the King Sigurd.

x.

" I love your fifter, wifh her for my bride;
" She muft go with me, feated by my fide,
" Her locks of gold will gild my old roof tree,
" And Alfsonnè fhall Sigurd's funfhine be."

xi.

Then fpake Alfblond-bart with a darkening frown,—
" Brief queftion needs brief anfwer, from our town:
" If fuch your objeét, go ye hence in peace,
" And Sigurd prithee let your love fong ceafe.

xii.

" In winter days, when fnow and hail fall faft,
" No rofe is gather'd; and in ages paft
" He was a favage who from home would tear
" A youthful maid—your wooing take elfewhere."

xiii.

Then ftood king Sigurd dumb, as turn'd to ftone,
Or as fome wretch is ftruck through blood and bone
By Odin's lightning; fhame to think that he
To whom all heroes bent the willing knee,

xiv.

Should be fo fcorn'd. Quick rufh'd the hot red blood
Up to his brow, and in his angry mood
So hard he prefs'd the gold and jewell'd cup,
That high towards heaven the wine flew fparkling up.

XV.

Then cried he, turning to the caftle wall,
" Farewell Blond-bart, and Eric Harfenfhall;
" Farewell fweet Alfsonn'—by my kingly word,
" Ye foon fhall learn how woos the king Sigurd."

HOW THE BROTHERS AND SISTER TOOK COUNCIL.

I.

LIKE flame in ftraw is youthful love and rage,
Like glowing iron is love and hate in age;
This fhall the two bold brothers fhortly know,
And golden-hair'd Alfsonnè to her woe.

II.

The time had come when 'neath the greenwood trees
One feeks cool fhade, and on the fummer breeze
Is borne the nightingale's fweet fong, when fped
To Alfheim in wild hafte, his fpurs all red,

III.

A knight, who cried—" With trumpet's fudden call
" Enragèd Sigurd bade his warriors all
" Bring horfes, chariots, and fuch warlike ftore
" On board his fleet, a hundred fhips and more.

The Ballad of the King Sigurd.

IV.

" And he has fworn a ftern and folemn vow,
" Ne'er from Alfheim to turn his veffel's prow
" Without Alfsonne.   Now council muft be held,
" With favouring winds his fails e'en now are fwell'd.

V.

Then fpake young Eric, " Swear I by my life,
" Our fifter ne'er fhall be king Sigurd's wife."
" It muft not be ; to dwell near ice would kill
" Our rofe."   Cried Alf, " confent we never will !

VI.

" Upon the blood-ftain'd heather will I lie ;
" More joyful far, more joyful fee her die,
" And breathe her frefh young life out up above,
" Than fee her wed a man fhe cannot love."

VII.

At a high cafement, fad with care they fpake,
Above the fea ; upon their fight now brake,
Like fwallows' flight, a mafs of fnow-white fail ;
'Twas Sigurd's fleet — fuch numbers muft prevail.

VIII.

On board the fhips the funlight flafh'd and glared,
On polifh'd coats of fteel, and fpears were bared
As thick as ears of corn in harveft days ;
With calm ftern eyes the brothers ftand and gaze.

c

IX.

They fought the upper room, where fat the maid
Alfſonnè, in her golden locks array'd,
Weaving a ſnow-white garment, as ſhe ſang,
Small ſilvery boats in the bright fabric ſprang.

X.

When ſhe her brothers ſaw, in haſte ſhe ſpeaks—
" Oh! what has chaſed the red blood from your cheeks?
". Sure no ſlight thing has cauſed ſuch ſudden fear."
Spake Alfblond-bart—" The king Sigurd draws near.

XI.

" Ten thouſand ſwords ſurround him as he lands,
" To force thee to his love he fierce demands;
" Reſiſt we cannot, ſince our force is ſmall:
" Who will thy honour guard ſhould we both fall?"

XII.

When they had ceaſed pale was Alfſonnè's face,
Some few tears dropt, (ſhe felt them no diſgrace,)
From her ſweet eyes, then ſpake ſhe—" Brothers dear,
" I know what is my duty, have no fear.

XIII.

" Alf's daughter would prefer death's cold embrace
" Rather than take in kingly bed a place
" By Sigurd's ſide. I have a deadly draught
" Which will, I thank the gods, not fail when quaff'd:

The Ballad of the King Sigurd.

XIV.

" My fole help now. Lo ! yonder on the ftrand
" I fee the helmets of his warrior band :
" Leave me awhile, my time is nearly come ;
" What one *muft* do is beft when quickly done."

XV.

With filent fteps ftrode Blondbart from the hall,
Kifs'd her upon the eyes brave Harfenfhall,
Left fhe fhould fee his tears, then all alone
They left Alfsonne. She made no idle moan,

XVI.

But ftept to a fmall fhrine, whence from a nook
A golden cup and filver flafk fhe took,
Within was magic juice of blood-red hue,
Which fome foul witch one moonlit night did brew.

XVII.

Out on the battlements fhe pafs'd, there lay
All round her gleaming hills and feas ; the day
Caft its laft beams on rocky heights and wood—
She ne'er had felt the world fo fair and good.

XVIII.

" Farewell," fhe cried, " oh, fun and day's fair light,
" Farewell, fweet fpring-time, my young life's delight ;
" No more in violet woods my fteps fhall ftray ;
" Farewell, fweet ftreams, which oft have feen me play.

XIX.

" Ne'er fhall I hear the gay birds fing again
" On bright May morn ; ah! ne'er fhall love's fweet pain
" Be mine.   I am fo young that life I crave—
" Oh, king Sigurd, why force me to my grave?"

XX.

The contents of the golden cup fhe drank,
Then heavy fell her eyelids, and fhe fank
With white cold lips upon the ground, her hair
Fell like a golden veil all o'er her there.

XXI.

Then ftillnefs fell on all furrounding things,
Daylight had vanifh'd, when a found of wings
Was borne upon the breeze, her falcon dear
It was, who came to feek his miftrefs here.

XXII.

When lying there fo ftill Alfsonne he found,
Three times he flew in wheeling circles round,
As if to wake her ; finding it in vain,
He foar'd out in the moonlit air again.

The Ballad of the King Sigurd.

How Alf and Eric were Slain.

I.

IN the cool morning hour, when the young day
All rofy cheek'd ftill on the mountains lay,
With clang of arms were Alfheim's meadows
    rife,—
'Twixt Alf's and Sigurd's men began the ftrife.

II.

Trembled the ground as horfes' hoofs rufh'd by,
Danced helmet plumes, and banners waved on high;
Hark how the fplinters fly from fpear and lance,
As clad in fteel the fquadrons quick advance.

III.

On fhields and coat of mail rang ftrokes of fword,
Clatter'd the fhafts like hail; the red blood pour'd
As ftreams let loofe; there wreftled mortal foes,
Till o'er the plain the duft in clouds arofe.

IV.

King Sigurd on a brazen chariot ftood,
In corflet of light fteel; with dragon's blood
His battle axe, two-handed, had, by aid
Of dwarfs, been temper'd; fire flafh'd from its blade.

v.

A vulture's head and claws of pureſt gold
Upon his helm he bore, bright to behold;
All o'er the battle plain at headlong ſpeed
Led by his voice, bore him his coal-black ſteed.

vi.

Ragnar his ſon rode by king Sigurd's ſide,
Surnamed The Grim; though ſtill in youth's ſpring-tide,
Already bearded; ſtrife he loved ſo well,
That loud he laugh'd as thick his fierce blows fell.

vii.

He ſang—" Upon the battle field there ſtands
" A hedge of roſes ripe for heroes' hands,
" Valhalla's gates ope wide for thoſe who fall,
" Then on, brave warriors! here I pledge ye all."

viii.

Into the thickeſt of the fight they daſh'd
At fiery ſpeed; their chariot wheels were ſplaſh'd
With foemen's blood: to Alfheim drove they on,
And through the ranks their ſword a paſſage won.

ix.

When Alfblond-bart king Sigurd's helm eſpied,
" Behold the creſt," to Eric then he cried,
" Of that fell vulture, who to her cold grave
" Brought our white dove: Ye gods, befriend the brave!"

The Ballad of the King Sigurd.

x.

With fword upraifed upon the king he fprang—
Ah! then how faft fell blows 'midft deafening clang,
As Blond-bart ftruck with his relentlefs blade
In mad defpair to avenge that injured maid.

xi.

In Sigurd's coat of mail he fpied a rent
Wherein to thruft, but fiercely Ragnar fent
A blow with his huge axe full at his head :
Crafhing he fell, his fair beard ftain'd with red.

xii.

Vanifh'd his life, clofed were his angry eyes,
King Sigurd o'er his body where it lies
Drove his war chariot towards Harfenfhall,
Who wild with rage had mark'd his brother's fall.

xiii.

And, rifing in his ftirrup, hurl'd his fpear
Full at the vulture's creft as it drew near ;
Quick turn'd the king afide, the lance but tore
The mantle which he on his fhoulder wore.

xiv.

In rage he drove his chariot at his foe,
Till he could aim two-handed one fell blow,
Then fwung his battle-axe aloft, till bright
Like yellow flame it flafh'd in the fun's light.

The Ballad of the King Sigurd.

XV.

Through Eric's bridle the fharp angry fteel
Cut to his horfe's neck; with fudden wheel,
Madden'd with pain, it gave one furious bound
And flung its mafter backwards on the ground.

XVI.

His foot ftay'd in the ftirrup, whilft his fteed
O'er all the field dragg'd him at frantic fpeed,
Trailing his light brown hair; his youthful head
Laid low : Alfheim's fweet maids will mourn him dead.

XVII.

When Alfheim's warriors faw their leader flain
They foon gave way; and o'er the battle plain,
Flinging away their arms, fled to the fhore,
Or to the diftant hills, and all was o'er.

XVIII.

King Sigurd on his horn now blew a blaft,
The fhrill note o'er the field had fcarcely paft
To call his warriors, when around they ftood,
Their coats of mail deep dyed in hoftile blood.

XIX.

In happy mood he hail'd them one by one,
And bade them feek the ftrand, then to his fon—
" My hero Ragnar, well thou beareft fteel!
" Now fhalt thou prove in fweeter toil thy zeal.

xx.

" The field is ours, and fee! the foemen flies :
" Now bring Alfsonn' to me, my beauteous prize !
" To-day I wed the maid in royal ftate,
" With eighty years there's little time to wait."

How King Sigurd celebrated his
Bridal Day.

I.

MIDST Sigurd's fleet, near that fell field of fight,
Lay moor'd a fhip, all deck'd in colours bright ;
The mafts and top-mafts built of wood moft rare,
Whence coftly pennons flutter'd in the air.

II.

Of fnow-white linen had the fails been made,
And e'en the cordage richeft filk difplay'd ;
Silver the anchor, and of bronze the helm,
Such was the bridal fhip—worth half a realm.

III.

Hard by, upon the fhore, king Sigurd ftood,
Purple his mantle, radiant in his mood,
Full of deep love for that fweet maid he burns,
Whom Ragnar fought. Ah ! joy to grief oft turns.

IV.

Forth from the caftle drew young Ragnar nigh,
As o'er the plain fome ftorm hangs in the fky,
E'er fierce it burfts in crafh and lightning's play—
So on his youthful brow dark horror lay.

V.

Seven armèd warriors follow'd him, who bore
A ftately bier with tapeftry thrown o'er;
Slowly they ftepp'd with awe-ftruck fadden'd eyes,
Greeting the king, whofe foul within him dies.

VI.

Then Ragnar fpoke—" Alas! bad news I bring,
" Like raven croaking muft I feem, oh king!
" Here is Alfsonnè, whom thy foul did crave,
" Thy bride fhe cannot be—fhe weds the grave."

VII.

He beckon'd to his knights that they fhould lay
Their burden down, then gently drew away
The hangings from the bier—as on a bed
Behold the lovely maiden pale and dead.

VIII.

She lay, 'midft lily buds, as if in fleep;
Clofed were her eyes, her cheeks their colour keep;
Clothed in white garments, of all jewels bare,
Her only ornament her golden hair.

The Ballad of the King Sigurd.

IX.

When Sigurd faw the maid lie cold as fnow,
He felt as if right through his heart a blow
Were dealt by two-edged fword: by heaven he fwore
That love like this he ne'er had felt before.

X.

No tears he fhed, but ftood with fad, fixed gaze,
And features fternly fet, as in amaze:
He look'd like marble image carved right well,
And filence deep through all the ranks there fell.

XI.

Long without motion ftay'd king Sigurd bent,
Then fudden raifed his head, and quick there went
A joyful flafh from out his eyes, and bold
He braved his fate, heroic to behold.

XII.

He faid—" The gods have work'd me grievous harm
" Thus to have fnatch'd my prize from this fond arm;
" That I am fpared it boots not them to thank,
" What's life to me fince my bright fun has fank?

XIII.

" For feventy years my fword I've borne in war,
" A hundred fights have feen my conquering car;
" Return I will not mourning to my hall,
" An old man fhorn of love, of fame, of all.

XIV.

" I fwore a folemn oath to heaven," he cried,
" Ne'er to go home without my lovely bride;
" Foul fhame it were to give that oath the lie,
" No! better far a kingly death to die.

XV.

" Now, warriors haften to the battle plain,
" And pile in heaps the bodies of the flain
" Upon the veffel's deck, 'tis meet that fo
" I to Valhalla with my comrades go.

XVI.

" Then gently lay Alfsonnè on her bier,
" Befide the helm, and brand of pine uprear;
" 'Twill feem, when kindled with its flaming light,
" As wedding torch fit for a nuptial night.

XVII.

" Ragnar, farewell! My brave, my hero boy!
" To thee I leave my crown with heartfelt joy;
" Farewell to all; now let the mufic play,
" And banners wave, 'tis Sigurd's bridal day !"

XVIII.

The fhip equipp'd, on deck the king calm ftrode,
No knight dare follow on that narrow road;
He loofed the cable, then the cords which held
The fails flacken'd, till in the winds they fwell'd.

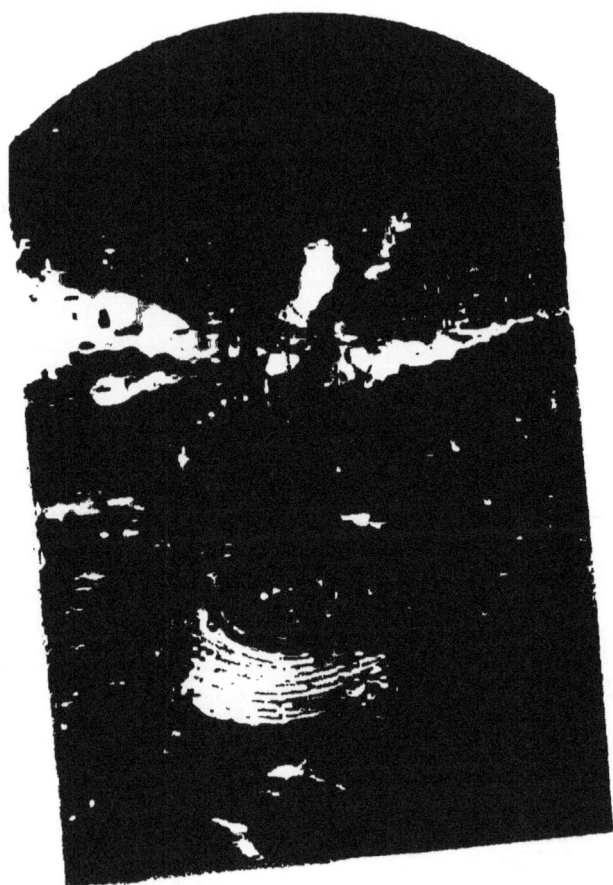

The Ballad of the King Sigurd.

XIX.

'Midſt muſic went the ſhip forth on its way,
As floats a dying ſwan at cloſe of day ;
On deck ſtood Sigurd, in his good right hand
The hero waved aloft a burning brand.

XX.

The leaping flames roſe mirror'd in the ſea,
Whilſt from the ſhore came ſtately melody,
Till ſhip and hero vaniſh'd 'neath the wave,
And thus king Sigurd found a ſea-king's grave.

BALLAD OF THE PAGE AND THE KING'S DAUGHTER.

(TRANSLATED FROM GEIBEL.)

PART I.

I.

THE King rides forth to hunt to-day:
  And 'midſt the foreſt trees
The hunter's horn, the hounds' deep bay,
  Are borne upon the breeze.

II.

And when the noontide pours its rays
  Through tangled buſh and brake,
The King's fair daughter ſlowly ſtrays,
  Nor knows which path to take.

III.

Softly ſhe rides, and by her ſide
  The Page with golden hair;
And were ſhe not a kingdom's pride,
  They were a lovely pair.

IV.

He looks on her, loud beats his heart,
    Crimfon'd are brow and cheeks;
They've reach'd the beech-trees' thickeft part
    When glowing red he fpeaks.

V.

" To hide my grief, it is in vain,
    Oh, Princefs, kind and fair;
My heart it breaks with love's fweet pain,
    Ah, liften to my prayer.

VI.

" If on that rofy mouth I might
    Imprefs one fingle kifs,
The worft of deaths would feem but light
    For fuch unhoped-for blifs."

VII.

She fays not " Yes"—no anfwer makes,
    But checks her palfrey's reins,
When from the faddle her he takes,
    His hand her foot fuftains.

VIII.

Down to the woodland's deepeft fhade
    They fteal and tell their love;
The nightingale fings in the glade,
    Murmurs the turtle-dove.

IX.

The wild red rofes bloom around
    Beneath the leafy fcreen;
The green frefh mofs ftrews all the ground,
    Meet bed for Love's foft Queen.

X.

Upon the mofly bank they ftay,
    And let their horfes rove,
Nor hear the nightingale's fweet lay,
    Nor horn wound in the grove.

XI.

Oh, hafte thee, King: the gold-haired Page
    Is by thy daughter's fide;
She, in his arms, forgets thy rage,
    The world, and all befide.

Part II.

I.

DOWN by the caftle of the King
    Two ride along the fhore;
    On high the winds their ftorm-notes fing,
The waves advancing roar.

II.

Then to the Page in accents dread
　　Thefe words the King thus fpeaks :
" Who gave thee, friend, that rofe-bud red,
　　That rofe thy hat fafe keeps ? "

III.

" My mother gave me this red rofe
　　When fhe farewell did fay ;
In water every night it blows,
　　To bloom afrefh next day."

IV.

Further along the winding creek
　　Still ride they fide by fide ;
The fea-gulls flying wildly fhriek,
　　Moans the advancing tide.

V.

When thus the King : " Boy, tell me true,
　　Whofe is that lock of hair,
Which, as afide thy mantle flew,
　　Lay on thy bofom bare ? "

VI.

" That is my fifter's light brown hair,
　　'Tis fweet as rofe's fcent,
With foftest filk it might compare,
　　She wept as thence I went."

E

VII.

Up the fteep rock their path now lay,
    Where, carved in letters rude,
Are Runic rhymes of olden days,
    When thus, in favage mood,

VIII.

A third time fpake the wrathful King:
    " Rafh boy, oh, tell to me,
Who gave thee that bright golden ring
    I on thy finger fee?"

IX.

" She who gave me this golden ring
    Her heart likewife fhe gives;
And fhe's the faireft maid, Sir King,
    Who in thy kingdom lives."

X.

Then, red with anger, cried the King,
    His eyes with fury burn:
" That ring—it is my daughter's ring,
    It's fparkle I difcern.

XI.

" And if, indeed, with wanton love
    Thou'ft dared my child to woo,
Thy youthful life no plea fhall prove,
    In death thy crime thou'lt rue."

XII.

Then to his heart with weapon keen
  He fmote him—nought can fave ;
His blood the Runic ftones between
  Flows downwards to the waves.

XIII.

Into the fea he did him fling :
  " And, fince thou aim'ft fo high,
Go, feek the haunts where mermaids fing,
  To win their queen, go try ! "

XIV.

To the King's caftle by the fhore
  One horfeman rode alone,
Whilft out to fea a body bore
  The waves with ceafelefs moan.

PART III.

I.

THE Runic ftones one fummer night
  Saw the mermaidens play :
'Midft rippling waters, breezes light,
  And moon in heaven which lay.

II.

They laugh, they fplafh, their arms they lave
'Mongft water-lilies fair,
Their golden locks float on the wave,
Gliften their white limbs bare.

III.

A fedgy bearded merman, through
A horn of muffel-fhell
Blows blafts to call the giddy crew,
But nought their mirth can quell.

IV.

Then cried the youngeft, laughing low,
" Ah, fee what I have here!
A gleaming body white as fnow,
Or filver fhining clear.

V.

" Upon a coral reef it lay,
I found it as I dived,
'Twas tangled in a branching fpray:
Say, what can be contrived!"

VI.

Around the body in a ring
They troop—their Queen thus fpake:
" So fair and fine this new-found thing,
A harp of it we'll make.

VII.

" Come, old Sedge-Beard, my trufty friend,
  Thou'rt wife in all things ftrange;
A fword-fifh thee for horfe I'll fend,
  So thou wilt work this change."

VIII.

The merman comes, the body takes,
  He labours fure and flow;
The pegs he of the fingers makes,
  Of the breaft-bone the bow.

IX.

He takes the Queen's bright golden hair,
  And with it makes the ftrings;
And foon the fummer night-winds bear
  Strange founds upon their wings.

X.

The harp he ftrikes with chords fo clear,
  The waves forget to moan,
The breezes hold their breath to hear
  That foft and wondrous tone.

XI.

The fea-mews fettle on the ftrand,
  The gold-fifh fwim around,
The winds and waters trancèd ftand,
  All charm'd by that fweet found.

XII.

The merman fings and plays all night,
　　Fatigue he doth not feel;
The mermaids dance, till morn's red light,
　　In many a graceful wheel.

PART IV.

I.

THE lamps flafh in the King's high hall,
　　The flutes and viols play;
　　The King's fair daughter leads the ball,
For 'tis her marriage-day.

II.

A myrtle wreath is on her head,
　　But ne'er a word fhe fpeaks;
Upon her breaft are rofes red,
　　But white as death her cheeks.

III.

All richly clad, with lordly air,
　　A Prince ftands by her fide;
But, oh! ten thoufand times more fair
　　The Page who for her died.

IV.

To paſs the wine, twelve maidens ſtand
    Around the board of gold,
And Pages ſwarm on every hand,
    Who wreaths and torches hold.

V.

When ſuddenly the lights dim burn,
    The viols ceaſe to play,
And from his throne the King ſpeaks ſtern,
    " What means this ſilence?—ſay."

VI.

" Before thy caſtle gates, Sir King,
    We hear the merman's lay,
When to his harp we hear him ſing,
    Our muſic we muſt ſtay."

VII.

And hark! from out the ſea there flow
    Into the feſtal hall,
Through the clear night, ſweet ſounds and low
    Which on their ears ſoft fall.

VIII.

The ſound into the bride's ſoul ſteals,
    As if in that ſame hour
Her dead love's preſence it reveals
    By ſome ſtrange magic power.

IX.

She knows not why, but from her eyes
    Faſt fall the tear-drops down;
Upon her breaſt the roſe-bud dies,
    Low lies her myrtle crown.

X.

To the King's proud ſoul it piercèd through,
    He curſed it in his heart;
The Prince to ſeek his charger flew,
    And hurried to depart.

XI.

With broken heart the Bride lies dead,
    For Grief hath power to kill:
And when the morning breaketh red,
    The Merman's Harp is ſtill.

CHISWICK PRESS:—PRINTED BY WHITTINGHAM AND WILKINS, TOOKS COURT, CHANCERY LANE.

www.ingramcontent.com/pod-product-compliance
Lightning Source LLC
Chambersburg PA
CBHW021445090426
42739CB00009B/1652